It's Different Now...
A New Beginning

Written and Illustrated
by

Carole D. Hillman Ed.D.

AuthorHouse™
1663 Liberty Drive
Bloomington, IN 47403
www.authorhouse.com
Phone: 1 (800) 839-8640

Published by AuthorHouse 01/23/2019

ISBN: 978-1-5462-4440-0 (sc)
ISBN: 978-1-5462-4441-7 (e)

Library of Congress Control Number: 2018906845

Print information available on the last page.

Any people depicted in stock imagery provided by Getty Images are models,
and such images are being used for illustrative purposes only.
Certain stock imagery © Getty Images.

This book is printed on acid-free paper.

authorHOUSE®

This book is dedicated to all
children everywhere.

Look at the cover pictures
and discuss them.

It's Different Now ...
A New Beginning

Note to Reader:

Decision making isn't always easy for any of us. There are some necessary thought processes that follow which facilitate using problem solving.

Mom and Dad used to be married.
We lived in a little red house.
I had a cat.
I had a dog.
I was happy.

One day Dad was deployed.
He did not come back.
I missed him.
I was not happy at all.
My sister hid and cried.

We moved to an apartment.
My cat went to a new home
My dog went away too.

Mom and I did not laugh much.
Sometimes Mom would cry.

I cried too.

I was sad.
So very, very sad...
So was my sister.

Mom decided to go back to school.
Someday she will be a teacher.
She took me to my own school.
I played with lots of boys and girls.

Each day Mom would give me a hug.
She would kiss me too,
She said, "I love you. Have
       a good day."
We all hugged!

We did not have a lot of
   good days after Dad left.
                    But....
Lots of time passed....

Mom laughs more now.
I laugh more too.
I think we are going to
    be happy again.
Only it's different now.

Mom calls it a new beginning.

This is space for you to utilize when you use your problem solving skills (Decision Making Skills).

This component is meant for the reader to contemplate and apply in a variety of contexts:

Consider this list of responsibilities.

You have:

...accepted a new job out of town, or... what might you do? Make a list.

...purchased a new or used automobile...

...accepted a date with someone new, or...

...enlisted in the army and have to ship out, or...

...cheated, or...

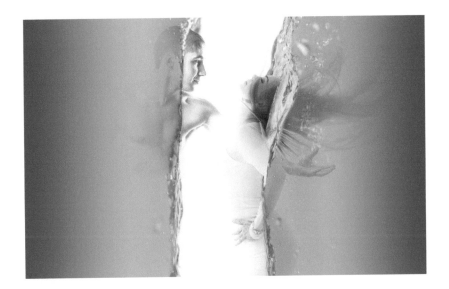

...lied...

Now...

Look at the list and choose one while making a list of skills, you need to develop and choose to use.

Try to go back through a "life skill test" and try to develop meaningful strategies to use in your future.

Now:
Pretend you are 6 years old and make a viable list of life skill possibilities.

Pretend you are a new parent, or a newlywed.

Are you noticing your problem solving skills?

Continue using positive decision making skills. Those are critical for strength and learning.

The more you do those tasks, the more you become less stressed and free.

Enjoy!

Examples or additional discussion:

Printed in the United States
By Bookmasters